Famous Firsts in Aviation

About the Book

Man's desire to fly has resulted in today's exploration of the outer atmosphere and space. From the first balloon, which rose majestically for the span of only ten minutes, to the intricate supersonic aircraft the history of aviation is filled with many astonishing "firsts." In his fascinating and well-illustrated account Jesse Davidson tells of man's lifelong inventiveness, his failures, and his great successes.

The *Famous First* books:

Famous Firsts in Sports
by John Jakes

Famous Firsts in Exploration
by Herbert Molloy Mason, Jr.

Famous Firsts in Baseball
by Joseph J. Cook

Famous Firsts in Medicine
by Bette Crook and Charles L. Crook, M.D.

Famous Firsts in Aviation
by Jesse Davidson

Famous Firsts in Space
by Gary Shenfeld

FAMOUS FIRSTS IN AVIATION

Jesse Davidson

G. P. PUTNAM'S SONS   NEW YORK

AUTHOR'S NOTE

Famous Firsts in Aviation offers a fair representation of outstanding and notable achievements which, in their time, came to influence the theories and concepts of aeronautical science thus bringing about the present state of the art.

The author concurs in the almost universally accepted view that Orville Wright was the first to fly under the conditions of controlled and sustained flight. At the same time he is aware of the claims put forward by those who maintain that the first to fly was, variously, Gustave Whitehead, Clément Ader, and Alberto Santos-Dumont.

Grateful appreciation is extended to David C. Cooke, author of many outstanding books on aviation, for his kind suggestions; to William J. O'Dwyer, Major, USAF Reserve, and Miss Stella Randolph, for the opportunity to study their records and Whitehead memorabilia; and to Stephen J. Hudek, aeronautical photo archivist, for his unstinting cooperation.

JESSE DAVIDSON

TO

Bette, Bruce and Carol Sue;
Glenn Richard and Laurie Tonsi-
Tonsi "W" — some firsts
of my own. And to Mollie G., for
the use of her typewriter and
kitchen table.

Contents

First Men to Fly

In 1783 the Montgolfier brothers, Joseph and Étienne, papermakers by trade, noticed how the warm air in their fireplace whisked charred bits of paper up the chimney. Intrigued, they held large paper bags open end down over the fireplace and released them. Instead of falling into the flames, the bags shot upward. In the act, they discovered that the trapped hot air made the bags rise because they were lighter than the colder air surrounding them. And so an idea was born.

Could a large bag filled with heated air carry a man aloft? The Montgolfier brothers pondered the question and decided to experiment. On September 19, 1783, their large heated air bag carried aloft a sheep, a rooster, and a duck. It drifted about 2 miles and came down gently some 10 minutes later, the menagerie none the worse. Aside from the natural flight of birds, these were the first creatures ever to fly. Now the question remained: Who would be the first *man* to fly?

On November 21, 1783, Jean François Pilâtre de Rozier, a physician and chemist, accompanied by François Laurent, the Marquis d'Arlandes, in a magnificently decorated balloon, rose majestically from the palace gardens in Paris. Any fears they may have had were quickly dispelled by the glorious view of the landscape below.

With the eyes of all Paris turned upward, Pilâtre de Rozier and D'Arlandes flew five miles around the city a few hundred feet above the rooftops. They came to earth about 25 minutes later, put out the smoldering fire in the charcoal-burning metal brazier, folded the bag, and hitched a ride home by more dependable horse-drawn carriage.

On June 15, 1785, Pilâtre de Rozier and his passenger P. A. de Romain went aloft in a hydrogen-filled balloon. Pilâtre de Rozier's attempt to combine the lift of hot air with that of hydrogen proved unfortunate. During their intended flight across the English Channel, sparks from the charcoal-burning brazier beneath the open throat of the gas-filled balloon ignited escaping hydrogen. The craft burst into flames, and both men perished—the first humans to lose their lives in flight.

In the first aerial voyage in human history Jean François Pilâtre de Rozier and François Laurent, the Marquis d'Arlandes, ascend over Paris in a magnificently decorated balloon. *(Smithsonian Institution)*

First Controlled Powered Airship

Without some sort of mechanical power, the gas-filled balloon could not be steered in any direction. At best, a balloon offered a one-way trip, and not always in the direction desired. The first break in this deadlock came in 1852, when Henri Giffard, a steam engineer, ascended from the Hippodrome in Paris on September 24 and sailed to Trappes, a distance of 17 miles, at an average speed of 5 miles per hour.

What made this flight different from those preceding it was the fact that his elongated craft was powered with a 3 horsepower (hp) steam engine (suspended in a cradle 20 feet below the gas-filled envelope) and turning an 11-foot-diameter three-bladed propeller. Steering was accomplished by a stiffened sailcloth attached to the end of a pole. While the engine did not provide any significant speed and the rudder was not fully effective, the combination of shape, propulsion, and guidance suggested greater possibilities.

About three decades later Captain Charles Renard and Lieutenant Arthur C. Krebs of the French Army Corps of Engineers designed and built a sausage-shaped balloon 165 feet long, under which was suspended a bamboo framework control car extending almost the entire length of the craft. Inside, a 9 hp electric motor powered by a series of lightweight batteries drove a 23-foot-diameter tractor propeller. At the rear of the control car were a large single rudder and a small elevator.

For takeoff, the craft was permitted to free-float high enough to clear surrounding obstacles, and then the battery power was engaged to spin the long shaft extending to the propeller. The large slow-moving propeller pulled the craft smoothly and quietly.

On August 9, 1884, Renard and Krebs flew their dirigible balloon, *La France*, from Chalais-Meudon in a circular 5-mile course at a speed of 12 to 14 miles per hour. This epic flight constituted the first in which a lighter-than-air craft was directed from and returned to its starting point.

Henri Giffard's steam-propelled steerable airship, 1852. *(Underwood & Underwood)*

Renard and Krebs' electric battery-powered dirigible, *La France*, 1884. *(French Embassy)*

First Controlled Flight in Glider

Otto Lilienthal, a German engineer, was at the threshold of attempting mechanically powered flight when he lost his life in a crash with one of his gliders. Lilienthal was born in 1848, and his boyhood was filled with the fascination of bird flight. His studies resulted in publication in 1889 of a book titled *Bird Flight as a Basis of Aviation*—one of the classics of aeronautical science. Though he maintained the belief that powered flight would be ultimately achieved by orthopteral (flapping wings) means, he began his experiments with a fixed-wing monoplane glider, making his first flight in 1891. By 1896 he had made more than 2,000 flights in various gliders built of willow wand and bamboo framework covered with waxed cotton cloth.

Racing down the incline of a built-up earth mound, his momentum created lift over the curved wing surfaces and, aided by the upswept air currents against the slope, managed to sail gracefully hundreds of feet. By gripping a bar of the framework, he was able to obtain a reasonable amount of control by shifting the weight of his body.

Lilienthal's almost-daily flights became widely known through the new art of photography, which enabled photographers to capture him in dramatic flight, and he thus received considerable exposure in journals and newspapers. In an attempt to reduce physical stress, Lilienthal attached a harness around his forehead which was tied in to the movable elevator. When he ducked his head, the elevator would point the glider upward; when he raised his head backward, the glider would nose down (a complete reversal of modern aircraft control systems).

At this point he was getting ready to use a cylinder containing compressed carbonic acid to actuate the wing tips in a birdlike flapping manner. Before he could put this device into operation, he met with fatal injuries on August 9, 1896, during a routine glider flight when a sudden shift of wind upset his balance.

Otto Lilienthal in a typical flight after a running start downslope, 1895.
(Underwood & Underwood)

First Rigid Zeppelin

As a young cavalry officer in the Prussian Army, Count Ferdinand von Zeppelin was sent to the United States in 1865 as an observer with the Union Army during the Civil War. There he saw the use of balloons to scan enemy positions and to direct cannon fire, and he made a number of tethered and free flights. His interest in lighter-than-air craft led him to studies for motorized airships, but it took another thirty years of frustrating efforts before he was able to finance and build his first rigid metal framework dirigible.

When the first huge, cigar-shaped airship was backed out of its floating hangar for its maiden flight on July 2, 1900, its 420-foot-long interior housed sixteen cells containing 338,410 cubic feet of gas. Twin 16 hp gasoline engines drove four propellers through chain transmission. Small rudders provided directional guidance, and a 550-pound sliding weight arrangement permitted fore and aft trim. There were many flights along the shores of Lake Constance, bordering Germany, Switzerland, and Austria.

Improvements in power plants and overall design followed, and within ten years Zeppelin was operating a five-ship airline in Germany. Between 1910 and 1914 the line carried more than 35,000 passengers without a single fatality. When World War I broke out, the German Army commandeered his airships for military use. Night bombing raids over England's coastal cities soon associated the name Zeppelin with terror from the skies. But when British fighter planes were able to climb high enough, airships became obsolete as a military menace.

The mid-thirties saw the return of the rigid airship for commercial purposes. Transoceanic flights of the huge *Graf Zeppelin* and its larger sister ship *Hindenburg* made air travel a luxurious experience. The era of the majestic queens of the air came to an end on May 6, 1937, when the hydrogen-filled *Hindenburg* exploded in flames as it hovered over the mooring mast at Lakehurst Naval Air Station, New Jersey, after a successful ocean crossing.

(Right) Maiden flight of Zeppelin LZ-1 over Lake Constance. *(Goodyear Tire & Rubber Co.)*

(Below) **End** of an era: the hydrogen - filled *Hindenburg* explodes at Lakehurst, 1937. *(Pathé News Film)*

First Heavier-Than-Air Powered Flight

SUCCESS FOUR FLIGHTS THURSDAY MORNING ALL AGAINST
TWENTY ONE MILE WIND STARTED FROM LEVEL WITH ENGINE
POWER ALONE AVERAGE SPEED THROUGH AIR THIRTY ONE MILES
LONGEST FLIGHT FIFTY NINE SECONDS INFORM PRESS HOME
CHRISTMAS   ORVILLE WRIGHT

Thus the message telegraphed from Kitty Hawk, North Carolina, on December 17, 1903, announced man's fulfillment of the dream of centuries. Few people knew of the hundreds of previous glider flights made by Wilbur and Orville Wright over the lonely windswept sand dunes of Kitty Hawk, where they unlocked the secrets of lift, stability, and control. And when the time had come for mechanically powered flight, they were confident. The brothers built their own engine and designed the propellers.

A coin was tossed. Wilbur called it. On December 14, lying prone, Wilbur piloted the airplane as it left the launching rail. It rose a few feet, stalled, and fell back to earth damaged. It was in the air just 3.5 seconds. Three days later, with the machine repaired, it was Orville's turn. Whirling propellers pushed the plane into the air after a 40-foot run on the catapult rail. Flying about 10 feet off the ground, he went a distance of 120 feet and landed safely 12 seconds later.

Three more flights were made the same day, the longest being 852 feet and lasting 59 seconds, before a strong gust of wind overturned their plane on the ground as the brothers were discussing the next flight. They secured the wreckage inside a shed and started out on a brisk 5-mile hike to send a telegram to their father, Bishop Milton Wright, of Dayton, Ohio.

Reports of their flights during 1904 and 1905 met with mixed reactions and even outright disbelief in this country and abroad. With quiet dignity, the Wrights chose not to challenge them.

A priceless photograph of a supreme moment in history. Wilbur watches as Orville pilots the "Flyer," December 17, 1903. *(Smithsonian Institution)*

First to Fly Across the English Channel

Louis Blériot was a self-taught pilot. He also had a reputation for being accident-prone. Although really never seriously injured in more than fifty mishaps, he had somehow mastered the technique of using the wing tips of his plane to cushion the shock of a crash.

When the London *Daily Mail* offered a 1,000-pound prize (approximately $5,000) in 1909 for the "first aeroplane crossing of the English Channel in any direction, between sunrise and sunset, by one of any nationality," the heavily mustached Frenchman happened to be at his lowest financial ebb. He had built a new monoplane to enter the race but lacked the money to pay for a special engine.

Help came to Blériot at the eleventh hour. While visiting friends, Mrs. Blériot saved the life of a young boy teetering perilously on a high balcony. That evening the grateful parents called upon the Blériots to express their profound gratitude. When the father, a wealthy Haitian planter, learned of Blériot's plight, he wrote out a check for 25,000 francs. Blériot gave him a receipt and promised him half the prize money should he win. Quickly his Model XI monoplane was readied at Barraques, near Calais, on the French coast, where Blériot awaited suitable weather conditions. While his competitors slept, Blériot awakened at 2 A.M, and by 4 A.M. he had made a brief test flight. The stars were still out, and the air was refreshingly cool. At 4:41 A.M. on July 25, 1909, just as the faint light of dawn broke, Blériot was off—across 26 miles of open water without even a compass to guide him.

Minutes later the new engine began to overheat and lose power. Providentially, a sudden brief rain shower cooled the engine, and it perked back to life. Through the shimmering haze he made out the cliffs of Dover and steered northward to Dover Castle, England. At 5:17 he plunked down hard on a grassy slope, breaking a propeller blade and collapsing the landing gear. Among the first to greet his arrival was the local customs official, who dutifully certified that the incoming Frenchman had nothing on his person to declare.

Louis Blériot (above) takes off from Calais, France, for Dover Castle, England, across the English Channel, 1909. Blériot (below) lands in Dover after the first air crossing of the English Channel. *(French Embassy)*

First Military Airplane

The Army's Bureau of Ordnance was skeptical of the Wright brothers' claim that their machine had military possibilities. When the French government tried to make a deal with the Wrights, the Aero Club of New York, alarmed because of foreign interest, prevailed on President Theodore Roosevelt to instruct the War Department to look into the possibilities of the Wright machine as a military vehicle. In December, 1907, the Aeronautical Division issued an advertisement for a machine "supported entirely by the dynamic reaction of the atmosphere and having no gas bag."

The advertisement called for a machine able to carry two persons, fly 40 miles per hour (mph) or better in still air, carry sufficient fuel for a flight of 125 miles, remain aloft for one hour without landing, and be able to return to its starting place without damage that would prevent it from taking off immediately for another flight. In addition, the machine had to be easily dismantled, transportable by horse-drawn wagon and capable of being assembled and readied for flight in about an hour.

There were forty replies to the advertisement. Of the three bids found acceptable, the Wrights' was one. Modifying one of their 1905 Flyers, they equipped it with a 32 hp engine and added other refinements. On September 17, 1908, during one of the qualifying flights, a control cable loosened, snapping a part of the propeller blade, and threw the machine out of control. Lieutenant Thomas E. Selfridge, flying as observer, died as a result of injuries sustained in the crash.

Less than a year later Orville Wright was back with an improved version and this time, with Lieutenant Frank P. Lahm on board, completed the final phases of the trial flights and even exceeded the specifications. This earned the Wrights a bonus of $5,000 more than the contract price of $25,000 for the machine.

The U.S. Army formally accepted the Wright machine as "Aeroplane No. 1, Heavier-than-air Division" on August 2, 1909. Two years later, after many mishaps and considerable repairs, the machine was restored to its original condition and placed in the Smithsonian Institution.

Wilbur Wright (wearing derby, above) holds wing tip as Orville (center) prepares to climb into seat. (At right) Orville Wright demonstrates the airplane at Fort Meyer, Virginia, 1909. (Both photos *Underwood & Underwood*)

First Seaplane

In 1906 Louis Blériot and his partner Gabriel Voisin were first to experiment with a float-equipped glider and a twin-propelled biplane, both of which failed to get off the water. But success came to their compatriot Henri Fabre, a marine engineer and navigator, who made it with one of the most impractical and weird-looking contraptions that ever took to the air.

Since he came from a family of shipbuilders, the sea was Fabre's first love. Yet with no previous knowledge of aerodynamics and never even having flown in an aircraft, he built his fragile craft around a set of three broad airfoil-shaped floats whose design contributed a measure of lift. The 28-foot-long body frame supported a wing with a span of 46 feet. A 50 hp rotary engine was attached to the rear end of the body. Sailcloth covered the lifting surfaces. A marine type of tiller was used to steer the plane's small rudders attached to the floats.

On March 28, 1910, he started the engine and planed across the water at 35 mph but failed to rise. On the second attempt he left a trailing wake 1,000 feet long before becoming airborne but rising no higher than 6 feet. On this first flight he traveled a distance of 1,600 feet.

On his fifth flight he was clocked at 55 mph and covered a distance of 3.75 miles. Fabre perfected his flying techniques with each succeeding flight and made improvements in float design.

In the United States Glenn H. Curtiss was first to fly a seaplane, the design of his floats bearing strong resemblance to those of Fabre's. Using them on his standard pusher-type biplane, he flew over San Diego Bay on January 26, 1911, covering a distance of 2 miles.

Henri Fabre sitting astride his Hydravion, the first seaplane to arise and
land on water, 1910. *(French Embassy)*

Straight and level, Fabre is clocked at 55 mph. *(French Embassy)*

First to Fly More Than 100 MPH

For the winner of an air race his victory meant fame and fortune. For the plane's builder, it meant staying in business. For example, after Blériot's flight across the English Channel in 1909 he received orders for 200 copies of his Model XI monoplane the following day.

In 1912 the Gordon Bennett Trophy race was being held in Chicago—the first time in the United States. The trophy had twice been won by Americans: Curtiss beating Louis Blériot for sheer flying skill and speed at the French air meet in 1909, and Charles T. Weyman, in 1911 at the British meet, flying at the unheard-of speed of 78 mph with a French-built Nieuport monoplane. But in 1912 the race became a contest among three Frenchmen: Jules Vedrines, Maurice Prévost, and André Frey.

The event started off at 9:30 A.M. on September 9. Vedrines flew the required 30 laps of 4.14 miles each, or 124.8 miles, in 1 hour, 10 minutes, and 56 seconds at an average speed of 105.5 mph. Prévost came in second with an average of 100.5 mph. Frey had to drop out when his Hanriot developed engine trouble after completing the twenty-third lap, though his average speed was 93 mph. Vedrines considered his winning "empty honors," for he was looking for real competition.

The American cup defender entry was a specially built Burgess monoplane, somewhat similar to the French designs. The Burgess plane failed to perform because there was *not one* qualified American pilot who had previously flown anywhere near the speed of 110 miles an hour that the airplane was expected to do.

The sleek Deperdussin racer being readied for flight. *(Stephen J. Hudek Aeronautical Archives)*

Jules Vedrines setting speed record in 1912. *(Stephen J. Hudek Aeronautical Archives)*

First Successful Flying Boat

"A large amount of equipment in the shape of aeroplane parts, machinery, and staff employees was sent recently from the Curtiss Aeroplane factory at Hammondsport, New York, to the Curtiss experimental station on North Island, San Diego, California."

Thus, in December, 1911, an aeronautical journal announced a flying boat which differed from Curtiss' previous pontoon-equipped pusher plane by its distinctive hull design. Between the bulkheads of the 20-foot-long hull was the cockpit, in front of which was bedded a 60 hp six-cylinder water-cooled engine and which, through chain transmission, drove counterrotating twin-tractor propellers. Other innovations included an engine self-starter, a fuel gauge, and a bilge pump.

The climate at North Island made it an ideal testing site. On January 10, 1912, the first hull type of flying boat lifted off the water's surface briefly after a long run. It was the first and last time this particular design did so. Further attempts were unsuccessful. The plane was shipped back to Hammondsport, and in the spring it emerged with a restructured hull, a new tail assembly, and an 80 hp engine mounted below the top wing in direct drive to a single pusher propeller.

Initial trials and high-speed taxiing failed to lift the new hull off the surface of Lake Keuka. Naval designer Holden C. Richardson paced the fast-moving hull in an accompanying motorboat to observe the churning wake trailing the raised prow. After several runs he suggested that a wooden wedge screwed to the bottom of the hull could possibly break the suction action that was holding the hull fast. Curtiss concurred. The precise date is not known, but sometime during the spring Curtiss flew off the water with amazing ease. After that there was no further trouble. Improvements in hull design of the Curtiss flying boats that followed served as the forerunner for the military and commercial flying boats for years to come.

Curtiss Flying Boat at San Diego, California, got off the water only once. *(Smithsonian Institution)*

Modified version was successful after Lake Keuka flight, 1912. *(Underwood & Underwood)*

First Four-Engine Airplane

Igor Sikorsky, a name synonomous with present-day helicopters, was a lad of fourteen when the Wright brothers first flew in 1903. Within ten years Sikorsky taught himself to fly, designed and built the first four-engine airplane, and personally flew it. His earlier efforts to build a helicopter failed, and this led him to concentrate on fixed-wing aircraft.

Sikorsky's dream to build a practical transport plane was realized after he was hired as an engineer with the Russian Baltic Company of St. Petersburg, manufacturers of railroad cars, farm machinery, and automobiles. In 1912 the company turned its attention to aircraft, and Sikorsky's first project was to design airplanes for entry in a military competition against other Russian-built aircraft of British and French designs. On September 28, 1912, the flying tests were completed, and two days later the Baltic Company was informed that Sikorsky's biplane, the S-6-B, had won a cash award of 30,000 rubles ($15,000). Given half the prize money, Sikorsky gratefully repaid his family for their financial support of his early experiments. Now he was free to construct his four-engine airplane—with the backing of his company.

As the airplane began to take shape, its large, unwieldy appearance caused foreboding. With the pilot seated in an enclosed cabin, a radical departure from the open cockpit, and with the ailerons and tail surfaces so distant from the control source, could this monstrous airplane fly safely if engine failure occurred? Sikorsky reviewed his calculations and maintained his contentions were mathematically sound.

On May 13, 1913, the 90-foot-span airplane with its four 100 hp tractor-pusher engines arranged in tandem on the lower wing was poised for flight. Inside the cabin were four seats, a sofa, a washroom, and a clothes closet. Because of the plane's sheer size, the four-and-a-half-ton craft was named the *Grand*.

With co-pilot and mechanic aboard, Sikorsky advanced the throttles. The big plane gathered speed and then lifted smoothly, climbing steadily at 60 mph. It was a good flight, but in subsequent flights Sikorsky considered a rearrangement of the engines, and in a modified version, they were placed as tractors, two on each side of the fuselage. On August 2, with eight persons aboard, the plane performed flawlessly.

Artist's rendition of the Sikorsky *Grand*, 1913. *(Sikorsky Aircraft Company)*

Rare photo of the *Ilia Mourometz*, the first four-engine seaplane, 1914. *(Sikorsky Aircraft Company)*

First All-Metal Airplane

In December, 1915, Professor Hugo Junkers designed and built a monoplane covered entirely with sheet duralumin. The craft was powered with a 120 hp Mercedes water-cooled engine. Even though Germany was at war and its air force was in a fledgling state, the Junkers plane was greeted with such skepticism that the military test pilot was ordered not to risk his life for the "crazy professor." On its first flight, the plane got off the ground in the amazing distance of 120 feet, flew low over the field, and, after a cautious turn, landed. There was no official comment from the military officials, but the professor was not discouraged.

The real trials of the Junkers J-1 began in mid-January, 1916. The plane performed well and reached speeds up to 100 mph. Still, the High Command was convinced that the metal plane had no place in Germany's military arsenal. They referred to the plane as the Tin Donkey.

With extensive modifications and weight paring, Junkers' next model, the J-2, using the original engine, flew 20 mph faster than the J-1. Again the plane was refused military acceptance, but this time the Army ordered a two-seater attack plane, specifically calling for a biplane—a dreadful design according to Junkers' philosophy. However, it meant staying in business. Retaining the basic wing design and construction techniques, Junkers came up with the J-4, a huge biplane accommodating a pilot and rear gunner and equipped with two forward-firing machine guns and one to protect against attack from the rear. Powered with a 200 hp engine, it performed so impressively that Junkers was given an order for 227 planes. But basically, Junkers was still a monoplane man.

Late in 1917 Junkers revamped the original J-1, which then became the J-9, armed with twin forward-firing guns. It was officially designated Junk D.1. No less than the great Red Baron himself, Manfred von Richthofen, top-scoring ace, flight-tested this plane and was so impressed by its spectacular climb to 16,000 feet in twenty-three minutes that he recommended its immediate production. Unimpressed, the High Command placed no orders for what would have been one of the war's most remarkable fighter planes.

After the war, in 1919, Junkers built commercial planes. His low-wing corrugated metal cabin planes became a familiar sight throughout Europe.

Despite the Junkers' performance during tests, the design was rejected. *(Stephen J. Hudek Aeronautical Archives)*

Heavily armored Junkers J-4 was first successful all-metal fighter. *(Stephen J. Hudek Aeronautical Archives)*

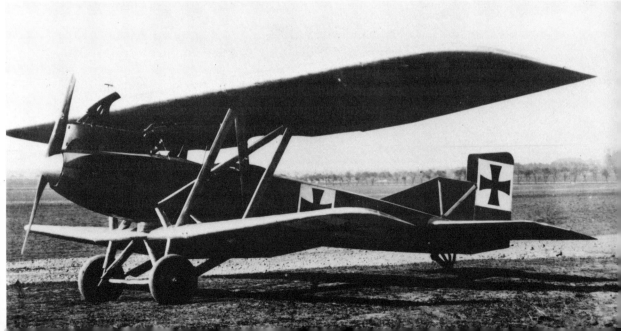

First Scheduled Air Mail

During World War I Assistant Postmaster General Otto Praeger was assigned the job of establishing daily air mail service between New York, Philadelphia, and Washington. His plan called for Army aviators to fly the mails, and May 15, 1918, was set as the inaugural date.

Almost everyone in high government positions knew of Praeger's plans —except those in the Army. And when they found out, they had exactly nine days in which to assemble specially modified trainer planes and assign qualified pilots.

Air Service Major Reuben H. Fleet, detailed to supervise the flying operations, objected to the short notice and begged for more time. "Aerial mail service starts May 15," he was told sharply, "and the President will be there."

Furious activity followed. Shortly before noon on May 15, Lieutenant George Boyle, who had been selected to fly the first trip northbound, strapped a map to his knee and signaled that he was ready to go. With President Woodrow Wilson, his wife, and many dignitaries in attendance, Boyle took off from Potomac Park in the nation's capital and soon disappeared from view. Twenty minutes later and some 20 miles away—in the wrong direction—the pilot came down to check his bearings. In landing, he flipped over, breaking the propeller. By curious coincidence, he came down on the farm belonging to Otto Praeger, in Waldorf, Maryland. The mail was quietly trucked back to Washington, and the newspapers never bothered to mention the incident.

In New York, Lieutenant Torrey H. Webb, flying out of Belmont Park racetrack, left on schedule and brought the southbound mail to Bustleton Park airfield, outside Philadelphia. The mail pouches were transferred to the plane piloted by Lieutenant James C. Edgerton, who completed the relay to Washington, thus making the trip complete.

The flight from Philadelphia to New York on May 15 was made by Lieutenant H. Paul Culver. Though the round trip was only 75 percent complete for the first day, U.S. airmail service has continued uninterrupted ever since.

Major Reuben H. Fleet (left) showing check points on map to Lieutenant George Boyle just before flight, May, 1918. *(USAF Museum)*

Takeoff with the first scheduled air mail in a Curtiss JN-4H from Potomac Park, Washington, D.C. *(USAF Museum)*

First Passenger Airliner

To France goes the credit for being the first nation to introduce the passenger airliner and to establish scheduled flights. Service started between Paris and London on February 8, 1919, with the twin-engine Farman Goliath biplane. Although it was a modified wartime bomber, the commercial version retained the same slab-sided body design, bluntly rounded nose and straight-edge high-lift wings. Accommodations varied, but typically the plane had two passenger cabins consisting of four wicker seats in the forward cabin and eight seats in the rear. Interior furnishings were spartan, and winter travelers sat bundled in their overcoats.

Service got off to a slow but dependable start. Improvements in comfort and decor came with each variant of the Goliath, reflecting the French taste for luxury. In demonstration of the transport's capabilities, pilot Lucien Bossoutrot, with four passengers aboard, coaxed the big plane to an altitude of 20,670 feet on April 1, 1919. Three days later this performance was repeated with fourteen passengers. On May 5 the Goliath outdid itself by carrying twenty-five passengers to an altitude of more than 16,000 feet in a flight of 1 hour and 15 minutes. When the British introduced their Handley Page twin-engine airliner on a parallel London-Paris route the same year, the Goliath set a nonstop flight record by flying from Paris to Casablanca, a distance of 1,274 miles, in 18 hours and 30 minutes. This achievement did much to help sell flying to the public, and the London-Paris route enjoyed an increasing patronage.

The Farman passenger transport put France on the airline map and was used by a number of other lines eventually to form Air Union, which pioneered the far-flung European routes.

The Farman Goliath carried eight passengers on Paris–London route in 1919. Pilots sat in open cockpit between wings. *(Underwood & Underwood)*

Extended routes brought about improved accommodations and service along with typical French cuisine. *(Air France)*

First Airplane to Span the Atlantic Ocean

To combat the German submarine menace in the North Atlantic during World War I, the U.S. Navy in January, 1918, placed an order for four large patrol planes with the Curtiss Aeroplane Company, whose experience with flying boats made it the logical choice. Eleven months later the war ended, and the Navy found it no longer needed the huge craft. Commander John H. Towers, who had been taught to fly by Glenn Curtiss, obtained approval from the Secretary of the Navy to have the NC (Navy-Curtiss) boats attempt a formation flight across the Atlantic. The ambitious undertaking got started in the spring of 1919.

Problems plagued the project from the beginning. Storm and fire partially wrecked the NC-1. Sister ship NC-2 was cannibalized so that its wings could be used to make the NC-1 airworthy again. By May 8 NC's 1, 3, and 4 roared out of the Rockaway, New York, Naval Air Station and headed for Nova Scotia, 450 miles away. Engine failure forced the NC-4 to land for repairs at Chatham, Massachusetts. The other two reached their destination without incident, but the next day discovery of serious cracks in the wooden propellers necessitated a layover for replacements. By May 15 the NC-4 joined the others at Trepassey, Newfoundland, the jumping-off site for the great adventure.

The following evening all three NC boats took off and headed into the gathering darkness over the watery expanse ahead of them, the evening hour departure chosen to enable the formation to land in the Azores during daylight. Below them, stationed at 50-mile intervals, Navy destroyers radioed weather reports to the NC's and were on standby alert for rescue service if necessary. By eleven o'clock the next morning the NC-3 was miles off course and low on fuel. Commander Towers ordered a landing, and the craft plowed head on into a big wave. The NC-1 was also having navigation troubles. Commander Patrick Bellinger wisely decided to land, and he put down without difficulty. Only Commander Albert C. Read and crew in the NC-4 remained aloft. After fifteen exhausting hours the plane came down at Horta, a small island in the Azores.

A Greek freighter loomed out of the fog and rescued the crew of the NC-1, which sank shortly afterward. The now-battered NC-3 managed to ''sail'' into Ponta Delgada harbor on May 19 with all on board. Finally,

The NC-4 starting across the Atlantic (above) and landing (right) in Lisbon Harbor, 1919. (Both photos *Smithsonian Institution*)

on the morning of May 27, the NC-4 flew from Horta to Lisbon, Portugal, landing on the Tagus River at twilight—the first airplane to span the Atlantic. After honors were accorded to the NC crewmen, the big boat flew on to Plymouth, England, 775 miles northward.

First Retractable Landing Gear

The first practical application of the fully retractable landing gear to overcome drag created by the conventional fixed gear, and thereby materially increase the speed and efficiency of the airplane, was proved in flight by the Rhinehart-Bauman RB-1 racer. The airplane was designed for entry in the last and final air race to be held in France in September, 1920, for permanent possession of the Gordon Bennett Trophy. A trio consisting of pilot Howard Rhinehart, chief engineer Milton Bauman, and engineer Charles H. Grant created the craft, whose radical departure from the norm placed it far ahead of its time. Compared to usual airplanes of the era, with their biplane wings, struts, wires, turnbuckles, control horns, and large drag-creating radiators, the RB-1 was the cleanest airplane yet built. With it was America's hope of capturing the coveted trophy.

The 22-foot-long fuselage was covered with three-ply wood veneer, as were the wings and tail surfaces. Manually operated controls from the enclosed cockpit actuated the linkage to vary the cambered sections of the leading and trailing edge wing slats and to retract the wheels completely within the oval-shaped fuselage. Pilot's visibility was gained through large transparent plastic windows on each side of the body. With its 250 hp Hall-Scott six-cylinder water-cooled engine, special wood propeller, and aerodynamic cleanliness, it was estimated the RB-1 would attain a speed of 200 mph.

Insufficient flight testing of the variable-camber wing caused the pilot some uncomfortable moments and temporary loss of stability, but a safe landing was always managed. Straightaway speed was spectacular. But steep banks and hairpin turns with the unproved wing created certain misgivings, and it was decided to withdraw the RB-1 from the final race.

Standing on exhibit in the Ford Museum in Detroit today, the airplane is an eye-gleaming reminder of the pioneering past whose distinctive features are very much in evidence in the present.

The RB-1, U.S. racing entry at the Gordon Bennett Trophy race, France, 1920. *(Stephen J. Hudek Aeronautical Archives)*

Lockheed Orion, first commercial transport plane with retractable landing gear. *(Underwood & Underwood)*

First Crop-Dusting by Airplane

In the early 1920's the boll weevil's devastating march on cotton crops threatened the southern American states with economic disaster. To meet this threat, insecticide, in the form of poison dust, was developed and dispersed by horse cart or tractor-drawn spreaders. Because of the tremendous acreage involved, a more efficient way was sought to combat the plague. Dr. Bert R. Coad, directing the activities of the U.S. Bureau of Entomology, studying insect control over sugarcane, tobacco, and cotton, recalled an Ohio forester had used an airplane to spread poison dust on insect-ridden catalpa trees.

Assisting Dr. Coad in his work was Charles E. Woolman, a young agricultural engineer, whose first love was aviation but who at the time found no immediate prospects in it for a livelihood. The men reasoned that perhaps the airplane could be brought in to fight the boll weevil. Dr. Coad went to Washington. His pleas before Congressional committees fell on deaf ears, but the Director of the Budget listened to the scientist and sent him back to Louisiana with funds and assurance of assistance from the Army Air Service.

With hoppers installed in the rear cockpit of two worn-out Curtiss Jenny trainer planes and an operator in each turning a hand crank, the planes flew back and forth a few feet above the cotton crops, spraying them with poison dust. The effects of insect control were becoming apparent when funds began to run out. Then fate brought George B. Post to Louisiana. He was ferrying a new airplane to San Antonio, Texas, when forced to land in a field adjacent to the site where Coad and Woolman worked.

Woolman was impressed with the sturdy-looking plane, its excellent forward visibility, and split type of landing gear. Post, however, was impressed as he watched the ancient Jennies work over the cotton fields, and the idea came to him suddenly. He was, after all, an airplane salesman, and if one man's meat was another man's poison, this was it!

Post flew back to New York and convinced his employers to set up an independent company to manufacture specially built crop-dusting planes and solicit this type of work. By 1924 the Huff-Daland Company had a fleet of eighteen planes engaged in dusting operations, laying swaths 45 feet wide and covering up to 500 acres per application.

Army Air Service planes such as this De Havilland DH-4 sprayed insecticide to combat the boll weevil in 1923. *(Underwood & Underwood)*

The modified Huff-Daland "Duster" specially designed for spraying, saved southern cotton and tobacco crops. *(Underwood & Underwood)*

First Nonstop Flight Across the United States

When the first attempt to fly across the United States nonstop looked as if it would end in failure on October 4, 1922, Lieutenants Oakley G. Kelly and John A. Macready, Army pilots, decided not to let their efforts go to waste. Swinging their big single-engine Fokker T-2 back to Rockwell Field, San Diego, California, from which they had taken off, they dropped a note to their commanding officer telling of their difficulties in getting the heavily laden plane above the mountain ranges before darkness set in. As long as they were in the air, they would attempt to break the world's endurance record. In this they were successful, coming down after 35 hours and 18 minutes to a tumultuous welcome.

On their second attempt from San Diego on November 2, they managed to clear the previous hurdles, and all went reasonably well until they reached Terre Haute, Indiana, where bursting cylinder jackets drained the water-cooling supply, causing the engine temperature to rise dangerously high. Lieutenant Kelly poured into the radiator all the drinking water, coffee, milk, and consommé he had on board. It helped somewhat, but when the fliers spotted the Indianapolis Speedway grounds, they decided to land while they had a field under them.

The third attempt originated from Roosevelt Field, New York, on May 2, 1923. When the 400 hp Liberty engine strained and showed no tendency to lift the ship from the ground, the takeoff was aborted, and the plane taxied to another position adjacent to Hazelhurst Field. The combined length of the two fields offered a runway almost 2 miles long, but between them was a 20-foot drop. Gathering speed, the lumbering plane bounced, rose a bit, settled, and bounced again. It was still earthbound as it dipped over the dividing line—miraculously becoming airborne but not climbing. Hazelhurst hangars loomed dead ahead. A man turned to his friend and said, "What fools those boys are. They'll never make it."

"I'll bet you five thousand even money they will," said the other.

The overloaded plane just seemed to flop over the hangar roofs, disappearing from view. Crowds gasped and ran to pick up the pieces. By the time the plane reached Coney Island 20 miles away it had risen to only 400 feet. After 26 hours and 50 minutes, Kelly and Macready landed in San Diego.

Lts. John A. Macready (left) and Oakley G. Kelly before their transcontinental flight. (*Underwood & Underwood*) Their overloaded plane (below) flew 20 miles before reaching 400 feet. (*Stephen J. Hudek Aeronautical Archives*)

Deluged with congratulatory messages, one telegram thrust into the hand of Lieutenant Kelly read: COLONEL FRANKLIN R. KENNY A FORMER EXECUTIVE OFFICER OF THE AIR SERVICE HAS WON A BET OF $5,000 ON YOUR FLIGHT WHICH HE TENDERS TO YOU WITH HIS RESPECTS AND BEGS THAT YOU ACCEPT IT. The fliers split the prize money.

First Air-to-Air Refueling

In the spring of 1923, Lieutenant Lowell H. Smith, of the Army Air Service, conceived a plan for inflight refueling that would extend the tactical range of bombers. Skeptics doubted that two planes flying in close proximity could maintain their course with safety for the length of time required to transfer fuel from one plane to another. Smith argued convincingly and got his chance. With Lieutenant Paul Richter joining him in the "receiver" plane, and Lieutenants Virgil Hines and Frank Seifert in a similar De Havilland DH-4 tanker plane, the foursome developed techniques until they had them down pat.

On August 27, Smith and Richter set out to establish an endurance record, the only practical way to prove their point. As their ship droned over San Diego, California, their initial fuel supply dwindled to the level where the first scheduled inflight fueling contact was to be made. At the precise moment, the tanker plane pulled into sight, rose above and slightly ahead, and at reduced speed, Lieutenant Seifert reeled out the 50-foot hose to the outstretched hand of Lieutenant Richter in the rear cockpit of the receiver plane.

As Richter touched the hose nozzle, he accidentally knocked open the release valve and was immediately drenched with gasoline. Luckily, the propeller slipstream whipped the fuel back, for had any of it spilled on the hot exhaust stacks of the Liberty engine, the fabric-covered plane would have become an inferno. It was a close call; but the transfer was successfully made, and this was followed by fifteen scheduled contacts during which time 50 to 100 gallons of gasoline were transferred without the loss of a single drop. Fighting fatigue and lack of sleep, Smith and Richter came down safely after establishing a record of 37 hours and 15 minutes.

Lieutenant Frank Siefert (holding hose) and Lieutenant Virgil Hines, pilot of the "tanker" plane. *(USAF Photo)*

Air-to-air refueling with Army planes in attempt to set endurance record in 1923 almost ended in disaster. *(USAF Photo)*

First Flight Around the World

During the early 1920's, aviators representing Britain, France, Italy, Portugal, and Argentina competed to be first to circumnavigate the world by air. All ended in failure. Then the U.S. Army Air Service decided to try and planned carefully for the effort.

Four World Cruisers were built by Douglas Aircraft Company. Each plane had a single 400 hp Liberty engine, a wing span of 50 feet, and could fly with either conventional wheel landing gear or seaplane floats. The crews of the four planes were: Major Frederick L. Martin and Sergeant Alva Harvey, of the *Seattle*; Lieutenants Lowell H. Smith and Leslie Arnold, of the *Chicago*; Lieutenant Leigh Wade and Sergeant Henry Ogden, of the *Boston*; and Lieutenants Erik Nelson and John Harding, Jr., of the *New Orleans*.

Leaving Clover Field, Santa Monica, California, on March 17, 1924, the World Cruisers flew to Seattle, Washington, where floats were installed on each airplane. On April 16, the official starting date, all four planes took off and headed north to Alaska. Then the problems began. The *Seattle* came down with engine trouble; the others made it to Dutch Harbor, Alaska, where they waited for the *Seattle*. On April 30, on its way to join its sister ships, the *Seattle* crashed into a mountain in dense fog, but the crew miraculously escaped injury. Eleven days later they trudged back to civilization. Lieutenant Lowell Smith replaced Major Frederick Martin as commanding officer.

The remaining three planes continued on, down the Alaskan Peninsula, across the Pacific, skirting Soviet territory and the Kurile Islands of Japan, thence to Shanghai, Hong Kong, Burma, Calcutta, Karachi, Istanbul. From there the planes flew across Europe. Off Scotland, the *Boston* was forced down at sea when its oil pressure failed, and the crew was taken safely aboard an American naval vessel. The *Chicago* and *New Orleans*, meanwhile, had continued their course to Iceland, Greenland, Labrador, Newfoundland, and Pictou Harbor, Nova Scotia. A new World Cruiser, *Boston II*, had been flown there to allow the original crew to complete the globe-girdling flight.

The planes arrived back in Seattle on September 28. Four had started out, three had returned, and two had flown completely around the world.

The Douglas World Cruiser *New Orleans* fitted for over land flights. *(USAF Photo)*

The *Chicago* with floats. Both planes completed world flight in 1924. *(Stephen J. Hudek Aeronautical Archives)*

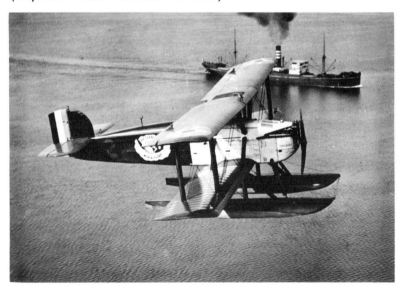

It took the *Chicago* and *New Orleans* 175 days, during which time they had flown 26,345 miles in 363 hours and 7 minutes, actual flying time. Among all planes, they had used twenty-five replacement engines.

First Popular Private Plane

After World War I great numbers of surplus U.S. military airplanes could be purchased for a few hundred dollars apiece. Ex-service pilots and civilian instructors bought them and turned gypsy, barnstorming around the country selling sightseeing rides, giving flight instruction, and performing stunts at country fairs and circuses. Any cow pasture served as the local airport, and it was under these circumstances that the helmeted and goggled heyday of private aviation got its start.

In Great Britain, however, surplus aircraft were not that easily obtainable. In order to encourage private flying, the Air Ministry held competitive trials at Lympne in 1923. Captain Geoffrey de Havilland, whose wartime fighters and bombers were widely used, saw the possibilities of a happy marriage between a scaled-down version of one of his military planes and an engine of compatible horsepower. He prevailed on his colleague, Major Frank Halford, to dissect a French-built eight-cylinder radial engine and come up with something of half the power and just as dependable.

Halford retained four of the original cylinders, pistons, and valves and mounted them on a new crankcase. The result was a four-cylinder in-line engine that developed 60 hp using an automotive type of carburetor and ignition system. In tests, the airplane exceeded expectations. It climbed 500 feet per minute, cruised at 80 mph, had a range of 320 miles, and landed at 30 mph. Its novel tow-and-go feature behind an automobile contributed to its ready acceptance by the growing flying fraternity. For nautical-minded sport fliers, the little biplane was equally at ease as a seaplane. It was christened the D.H. Moth.

The DH *Moth* introduced personal sport flying to Europe in the mid-twenties. *(Hawker Siddeley)*

The versatile *Moth,* equally at home on floats, was popular in the U.S. and Canada in the late twenties. *(Underwood & Underwood)*

First Rocket-Propelled Manned Flight

Chinese legend maintains that a learned official named Wan-Hoo, who lived around A.D. 1500, was the first human to fly. He did this, so the legend goes, by constructing two huge kites and joining them together with a bamboo framework, in the center of which was installed a saddle type of seat. Forty-seven large gunpowder-filled rockets were attached to the framework at strategic points. When he took off in a cloud of smoke he never was heard from again.

Actually Friedrich Wilhelm Stammer made the first rocket-propelled man-carrying aircraft flight on June 11, 1928, in Wasserkuppe, Germany. Aided by means of a rubber rope and the simultaneous firing of one of two solid-fuel rocket charges, the glider flew straight for about 200 yards. Stammer described the rest of the flight this way:

"I noticed a slight climb. I made a curve of about 45 degrees to the right and flew another 300 yards. Then I turned again to the right about 45 degrees. Immediately after the second turn the first rocket ceased burning and I ignited the second. This time I flew about 500 yards in a straight line, made a turn to the right of about 30 degrees and landed the machine after another 200 yards, just a few seconds before the second rocket was exhausted."

Stammer covered about a mile, and the flight lasted just over a minute. The flight, he said, had been "extremely pleasant," and he added, "I had the impression of merely soaring. Only the loud hissing sound reminded me of the rockets."

Fritz von Opel, who sponsored the first flight, made the second rocket-propelled flight at Frankfurt, Germany, on September 30, 1929, when he flew 1.25 miles in as many minutes at an altitude of 50 feet. The craft was wrecked on landing, but he escaped unhurt.

Fritz von Opel in his rocket-propelled glider at Frankfurt, Germany, 1929.
(David C. Cooke)

First Airplane Deicers

One night it "rained ducks" over Thief River, Minnesota. It happened during the year's first sleet storm. All night long the seasonal flight could be heard honking overhead. Then, about 4 A.M., the ducks began dropping in. Thousands of them crashed into the streets and buildings. Ice had coated their wings and forced them down. Airplanes faced the same problem in the early days of aviation.

Pondering this difficult aeronautical problem, Dr. William C. Geer of Ithaca, New York, began to experiment with ice adhering to a base of rubber. When the rubber base was stretched, the ice did not stick. With the cooperation of the B. F. Goodrich Company and the able assistance of a young engineer named Russell S. Colley, a refrigerated wind tunnel was built in which simulated tests on model plane wings proved that a small accumulation of ice on the leading edge of wings changed their profile, acted as a spoiler, and resulted in a loss of lift.

A possible solution suggested that a change of base adhesion, combined with a changing shape, would permit the airstream to get under the ice, dislodge it, and in effect serve as a deicer. This brought about the invention of the deicing boot, which consisted of long rubber strips attached to the wing's leading edge. Tubes inside the boot could be inflated and deflated by air pressure in regular pulsation. This flexing action (like bending a rubber tray with ice cubes in it) would crack the ice, which in turn would be blown away by the windstream.

The first test was made in a Douglas biplane with veteran pilot Wesley L. Smith at the controls and Russ Colley sitting on a "soap box" in the forward mail compartment, both wearing parachutes. When they found a freezing zone and picked up ice, Colley, working furiously, operated a bicycle hand pump with a two-way valve to alternate the inflation of the three tubes running the length of the boots on each wing. Bracing wires began to sag under the weight of the ice and set up dangerous vibration. The metal propeller picked up ice and threw it off unevenly, making matters rough on the powerful engine. But the pulsating tubes worked successfully, and the ice particles slithered off. The next step resulted in mechanically operated inflatable tubes.

When the biplane gave way to the monoplane, wires were no problem.

Engineer Russell L. Colley (left) and mail pilot Wesley L. Smith after successful deicing tests over Cleveland. *(B. F. Goodrich)* Rubber deicer boots (below) on leading wing and tail surfaces of DC-3. *(Eastern Air Lines)*

And as fabric-covered wings gave way to metal, new deicer boot attachments were devised. On larger transport planes electrically heated surfaces prevented ice accumulation just as effectively.

First Controllable-Pitch Propeller

The fixed-pitch wood propeller, for years the mainstay of the airplane it was designed to propel, and its immediate successor—the two-position ground-adjustable steel-bladed propeller—had reached the peak of their efficiency. If progress was to be made in commercial aviation calling for larger and faster transport planes, propeller development had to keep pace.

In 1930 the Hamilton Standard Propeller Company, in Connecticut, brought out a controllable-pitch propeller that enabled the pilot practically to "shift gears" in the air by setting the blade angles at low pitch for takeoff and climb and at high pitch for level flight and most economic cruising. This was accomplished through the use of a hydraulic pressure-operated mechanism in the propeller hub which changed the blade angle to meet specific speed, load, and attitude requirements.

The practicability of the controllable-pitch propeller was regarded as one of the most revolutionary advances in aviation. It won for Hamilton Standard the Collier Trophy for 1933, annually awarded by the National Aeronautic Association for the greatest achievement in aviation. When United Airlines compared performances between the ground-adjusted and controllable-pitch propellers on their twin-engine Boeing 247 transports, the latter's performance was so superior that immediate replacement was ordered for the entire fleet.

About this time Douglas Aircraft was coming up with the first of the DC (Douglas Commercial) series and designed its line on the basis that Hamilton Standard would come through with a three-bladed controllable-pitch propeller in time to meet its requirements. This Hamilton Standard did—and more. In 1935 it came out with the first constant-speed control propeller which automatically changed its blade angle for best flight conditions. In 1938 it developed the hydromatic quick-feathering propeller.

DC-3 (above) with right engine stopped and propeller in full feather position. (Right) Ryan FR-1 Fireball fighter— a combination piston-powered and jet engine —flying on jet power alone. *(Underwood & Underwood)*

First Pressurized Transport Plane

In terms of aircraft development, commercial companies were, in most cases, first to propose systems or components adaptable to military needs. The case was reversed in the mid-thirties when the Army Air Corps, after doing its own research in high-altitude flying in the region of the substratosphere—about 7 miles up—asked the Lockheed Aircraft Company of Burbank, California, to build a modified version of its twin-engine Electra capable of holding pressure in its cabin.

Starting in June, 1936, the Lockheed XC-35 was built in secrecy, its nearly spherical fuselage designed extra strong to hold a 10-pound-per-square-inch differential between the inside and outside pressure—a differential that meant that nearly three-quarters of a ton of bursting pressure would be exerted on each square foot of cabin area. Neoprene sealing tape and pressure-resistant Plexiglas windows were installed to ensure leakproof security. When the fuselage was completed, Lockheed applied the maximum pressure. Not a single rivet popped!

Dubbed the Boiler, the XC-35 made its first flight on May 7, 1937, and was turned over to the Air Corps in August. The supercharged cabin, in which even pressure was maintained at all times, eliminated the need for inflight oxygen face masks necessary on previous unpressurized planes. On one trip from Chicago to Washington, D.C., the XC-35 averaged more than 350 mph above 20,000 feet, though its top speed at sea level was just over 200 mph.

In 1939 the first fully pressurized airliner to go into commercial service was the four-engine forty-passenger Boeing 307 Stratoliner operated by TWA. Its entire fuselage was practically an airtight cylinder capable of withstanding an internal pressure of 6 pounds per square inch. Fresh air drawn through ducts in the leading edge of the wings was compressed by engine-driven superchargers and under temperature control circulated throughout the cabin. Spent air was discharged via an exhaust chamber located below deck.

Design of the substratosphere Lockheed XC-35 won Collier Trophy for Army Air Corps in 1937. *(Underwood & Underwood)*

World's first altitude-conditioned airliner was Boeing Stratoliner, forerunner of present high-flying jets. *(TWA)*

First Jet-Powered Airplane

Dr. Ernst Heinkel, a German airplane manufacturer, saw great potential in the idea of a jet-reaction engine brought to his attention in 1936 by a young physicist, Hans Pabst von Ohain. Heinkel hired Von Ohain to build a working model. Then, when Heinkel learned that his competitor, Junkers Aircraft, was also involved in reaction-type propulsion experiments, he put the pressure on Von Ohain, who was thinking in terms of years of development. Heinkel was thinking in terms of months! Von Ohain soon learned why. In another part of his plant, Heinkel was quietly building fuselages to test rocket engines devised by another brilliant young engineer, Wernher von Braun. Heinkel wanted to be first with *two* new exciting forms of aircraft propulsion.

In March, 1937, Von Ohain and his assistant, Max Hahn, completed the first test-stand engine. They started the compressor blades with an auxiliary motor, and when it attained some thousands of revolutions per minute (rpm), they turned on the liquid-hydrogen fuel supply and flicked the ignition switch. The engine blasted into a flame-producing roar and as the rpm's increased, the auxiliary motor was disengaged. No drops in the rpm's followed. The jet was running on its own.

Elated, Heinkel ordered the immediate production of a flight engine. (Von Ohain pleaded combustion problems and for more time and predicted that gasoline would produce more power.) In the meantime, the Heinkel He 176, whose wing and body measured only seventeen feet, was fitted with a 500-pound-thrust rocket engine. At 6:53 A.M. on June 30, 1939, Luftwaffe test pilot Erich Warsitz fired up the engine and was off on the first liquid-fueled rocket-powered flight in aviation history. Two minutes later he was safely down. The following day the He 176 was demonstrated before high-ranking Luftwaffe officers. One general expressed horror at flying so dangerous a craft; another general promoted Warsitz to a captaincy on the spot—for bravery! Only Hermann Göring, chief of the Luftwaffe showed some enthusiasm for a little propellerless plane squatting nearby on static display.

In mid-August an improved turbojet engine of 1,100-pound-thrust was mated to the Heinkel He 178 in a closely guarded hangar. At 4 A.M. on August 24, 1939, the fire-belching plane thundered into the air, flying

The Heinkel He 178, first military jet, was not the well-kept secret the Germans hoped it would be. *(Warren M. Bodie)*

smoothly despite the fact that its landing gear failed to retract. Fifteen minutes later Warsitz rolled to a stop, narrowly averting a high-speed landing mishap. Out stepped the first man to fly both a liquid-fuel rocket and turbojet airplane.

First Practical Helicopter

Credit for accomplishing the first VTOL (vertical takeoff and landing) —the basic concept of helicopter flight, using rotating wings—still remains unresolved, based on a technicality. The crux of the matter is that two Frenchmen succeeded in getting their respective machines off the ground under somewhat similar circumstances.

The first, according to French aeronautical records, was the manned Breguet-Richet machine which, on September 29, 1907, ascended less than 6 feet. However, it was stabilized by four men holding tethering poles "because the craft was not considered fully controllable." Two days before the Breguet's flight, Paul Cornu's helicopter, unmanned but tethered, carrying a 110-pound bag of soot in the pilot's seat, lifted several inches clear of the ground.

On November 13, 1907, Cornu in his helicopter lifted unrestrained about two feet, for a period of 20 seconds—the first time anyone had left the surface of the earth using lift created by rotating wings. Aviation historians generally acknowledge Cornu's accomplishment on November 13 as the first free direct-lift flight. But development between the theoretical design and the practical aircraft had yet a long way to go.

On June 26, 1936, the German Focke-Wulf Fw 61 Achgelis, using a conventional airplane fuselage, engine, propeller, and tail surfaces, achieved helicopter capability through the use of drive shafts extending sidewise from the engine to rotor blades mounted on outriggers on each side of the fuselage. True helicopter flight is accomplished by the main lifting rotors that provide up, down, forward, backward, and side movement through cyclic pitch action.

All these characteristics were eventually harnessed in Igor Sikorsky's VS-300 helicopter. Following a number of modifications which also improved the awkward-looking structure's appearance, Sikorsky's efforts came to fruition on May 6, 1941, when he established a world helicopter endurance record of 1 hour, 32 minutes, and 26 seconds. In the light of its development and practical versatility, the Sikorsky helicopter is acknowledged as the progenitor of all modern rotary-wing aircraft.

Paul Cornu's helicopter (above), carrying two men and weighing 739 pounds, hovered under control for one minute. *(Stephen J. Hudek Aeronautical Archives)* First successful helicopter (right) designed and built by Igor Sikorsky in 1939. *(Sikorsky Aircraft Company)*

First to Fly Faster Than the Speed of Sound

On October 14, 1947, the Bell XS-1, a rocket-powered airplane whose body was shaped like a bullet, made history by flashing through the skies faster than the speed of sound. Flown by U.S. Air Force Captain Charles E. Yeager, the plane attained a speed of 760 mph. When the fact was announced to the world, it was quickly acclaimed as second in importance only to that of the first flight of the Wright brothers.

A short time later Yeager boosted his record to 956 mph. His feat was truly heroic, for he had no means of escape from his plane. There had been widespread belief among experts that an aircraft attempting to penetrate the so-called sound barrier would disintegrate. But the XS-1 (Experimental Supersonic One) slid through the barrier with only a slight buffeting.

Development of the X-series research planes began after reports that some World War II conventional fighter planes had reached such high speed in dives that they became uncontrollable and broke apart. Aeronautical scientists agreed with the National Advisory Committee for Aeronautics that if a jet-propelled plane attained the same high speeds in level flight, it would provide valuable aerodynamic information.

Three X-1's, each slightly different, were ordered from the Bell Aircraft Company of Buffalo, New York. By 1945 rocket engines became available, and they were substituted for the originally planned jet. Titanium, lighter than steel, was used for the fuselage and wings to resist the great heat that would be generated by the friction the air produced beyond Mach 1—the speed of sound, 740 mph at sea level.

The XS-1 was flown until January, 1952, after which it was retired until 1954. In modified form it came back as the X-1E in 1955. In the meantime, Captain Yeager flew the X1-A, another improvement of the XS-1, this ship having an emergency ejection seat. On December 12, 1953, the X-1A flew at more than twice the speed of sound (Mach 2.435), or 1,650 mph. With Major Arthur Murray at the controls, the machine set a new altitude record of 90,000 feet on June 4, 1954.

The Bell X-1 (right) was designed for jet propulsion and modified to take rocket engines. The X-1 (below) flying on rocket power. *(USAF Photos)*

First Jet Passenger Airliner

Great Britain's wartime experience with jet engines enabled that country to take the lead when the feasibility of commercial jet transportation became apparent. Until 1952, when the first De Havilland Comet jet liner went into European service, the United States led the world in air travel with its famed Douglas DC planes, Boeing Stratocruisers, and Lockheed Constellations. The final design for the Comet I was completed in 1947, a scant two years after World War II.

When the Comet was rolled out of its hangar for tests on April 2, 1949, its glistening metal finish, sleek profile, and swept-back wings, noticeably void of engines and propellers, made it a beauty to behold. In flight it was swift and graceful. On May 2, 1952, the first jet passenger service was established by BOAC between London and Johannesburg, introducing fast, comfortable, almost vibrationless flight.

Exactly one year later tragedy struck. A Comet broke up in a storm after leaving Calcutta. All Comets were grounded, and some sixty precautionary modifications were made covering every suspected cause. Eight months later another Comet came apart in midair. Both machines had fallen irretrievably into the sea. British technological prestige had been dealt a shattering blow. Before a shocked nation had a chance to recover, another Comet disintegrated in clear skies high above the Mediterranean. Though the wreckage had settled beyond the normal reach of divers, a determined Royal Navy brought in its most sophisticated devices to bring up vital clues. The cause was metal fatigue which weakened areas of the cabin. Explosive decompression came like a powerful bomb.

The British Air Ministry made its findings available to the world's aeronautical industry. De Havilland continued to build newer and stronger Comets, many of which are still in service. During this time the American-built Boeing 707 four-engine jet liner became almost universally adopted by the free world's airlines.

First production De Havilland Comet (nearest camera) in flight with two prototypes. *(Hawker Siddeley Photo)*

First Nonstop Flight Around the World

It was only two nights before the mission that the crew of fourteen learned of their ultimate destination. A well-kept secret involving long and careful preparation by the Strategic Air Command of the U.S. Air Force called for a B-50 Superfortress bomber to make a nonstop flight around the world for the purpose of proving that midair refueling of American bombers would enable them to strike defensively anywhere in the world.

The four-engine Boeing B-50, a larger, heavier, faster, and more powerful version of the Boeing B-29, its look-alike predecessor which brought devastation to Japan in World War II, was the peacetime backbone of SAC. But it had yet to demonstrate its striking capability. For its global mission extra fuel tanks were installed in the bomb bays. Orders for the flight came through at 7 A.M. on February 26, 1949. At 11:21 A.M. the 140,000-pound bomber was airborne after a 6,000-foot run from Carswell Air Force Base, Fort Worth, Texas.

Pilots Captain James G. Gallagher, Lieutenant Arthur Neal, and Captain James Morris spelled one another at the controls as the plane headed eastward across the United States and out over the Atlantic. Fifteen and a half hours later two tanker planes arose over the Azores to meet *Lucky Lady II* and refuel her. Aided by a brisk tail wind, the ship arrived over Dhahran, Saudi Arabia, two hours ahead of schedule, where it made its second contact. While flying across India and toward the Bay of Bengal on its way to Manila, the third refueling point, everything was running so smoothly that Lieutenant Neal wrote in his flight log, "This is one sweet airplane." Over the Philippines a transfer was made, and there was a last contact over Johnston Island. Now it would be a downhill flight—if everything continued to go well.

Plowing through massive cloud formations, *Lucky Lady II* droned on monotonously high over the Pacific until the crew spotted the lights of Los Angeles just before dawn. "By God, we *are* going to make it!" said aircraft commander Captain Gallagher. Over Arizona, three B-29's joined *Lucky Lady II* in a welcoming escort to Carswell, where the globe-girdling bomber made the traditional sweeping pass over the field signaling "Mission Accomplished." Touchdown came at 9:31 A.M. on March 2, 1949, 23,452 miles, 94 hours and 1 minute after takeoff.

Lucky Lady II (with diamond insignia) being refueled by B-29 tanker during practice mission over Arizona. *(USAF)*

Seconds before touchdown, *Lucky Lady II* arrives at Carswell AFB, Texas, completing nonstop flight around the world. *(USAF)*

First Winged Aircraft into Space

As an outgrowth of experimental projects involving earlier supersonic X-series aircraft, an industry-wide competition was held in the United States following design studies initiated in 1952 by the National Advisory Committee for Aeronautics (now the National Aeronautics and Space Administration). The U.S. Air Force and the U.S. Navy were seeking a manned aircraft capable of hypersonic speeds and reaching an altitude of at least 264,000 feet. The purpose was to explore flight at the limits of the earth's atmosphere, obtain data on thermal aerodynamics, weightlessness and its physiological and psychological effects on man, and the effectiveness of jet-reaction controls associated with space maneuverability and reentry into the atmosphere.

The answers provided by the half missile, half airplane designated the X-15 were vitally necessary before a man could be lofted in a space capsule atop a rocket-powered missile, orbit the earth, and return safely. In December, 1955, the North American Aviation Company won a contract to construct three X-15's. On September 17 in an air-lifted rocket-powered flight company test pilot Scott Crossfield hit 1,350 mph and climbed to 52,341 feet.

From March 25, 1960, when NASA and military test pilots took over the flight programs, speed and altitude records fell one after another during a steady progression of fact-finding exploratory flights. On April 30, 1962, the X-15 was taken up to 45,000 feet over Mud Lake, Nevada. Released from the mother ship, it dropped 1,450 feet, and then NASA pilot Joe Walker ignited the rocket engines. With more than twice the horsepower of the Navy's largest aircraft carrier at his command, he blasted the X-15 upward at a speed of 2,760 mph to an altitude of 142,000 feet after a rocket burn of 82 seconds. Shutting down the engines, Walker continued on course upward in a fixed arc like a cannon shell to an altitude of 246,700 feet. There, in the region of space, he and his aircraft were weightless. Instead of tumbling and twisting about, the X-15 was under complete control. Twelve miniature thrust rockets (composed of hydrogen peroxide), spurting from little holes around the nose and under each wing tip when triggered by the pilot, enabled him to guide the plane in any direction.

Dwarfed by the size of the B-52, the X-15 nestles under the wing preparatory to be dropped from high altitude. *(USAF)*

When the X-15 program ended in November, 1968, the winged spacecraft under Joe Walker had reached its highest altitude, 345,200 feet (67.08 miles) on August 22, 1963. With W. J. Knight at the controls, the X-15 reached its highest speed, 4,534 mph (Mach 6.72) on October 3, 1967. Air Force test pilots who flew the X-15 at altitudes above 50 miles were designated as astronauts.

Index

The Author

JESSE DAVIDSON, born in Passaic, New Jersey, started flying in 1939. He has written several books and numerous magazine articles ranging from how to build rubber band and gasoline engine powered model airplanes to discussions of the industries related to aircraft. At present his hobby is gliding and soaring in the Catskills.